A Payment History
of the
United States

Kaz Nejatian, CEO of Kash

I dedicate this book to all retailers everywhere; especially my favorite retailer, my mother.

CONTENTS

INTRODUCTION

Money is an odd, odd thing. It is hard to understand how it works; and you don't have to be an economist to know that money is complicated.

Just turn on the radio. After love, the most complicated subject of all, money is the second most popular topic among the people writing the songs that we all love.

Money is so complicated that it is easier to rhyme the words to Notorious B.I.G's "mo money, mo problems" or to sing Liza Minelli's "money makes the world go around" on key than it is to describe what money actually is.

If you ask an economist what money is, they will be able to answer you very quickly. They will tell you, money is anything that can fulfil three functions:

1. A store of value: a thing that people can save and use later, something that doesn't just expire or disappear if you hold on to it.
2. A unit of account: a thing based on which

everyone can measure the value of other things

3. A medium of exchange: a thing that people can use to transfer value to one another. More easily, a thing that people can use to buy things, pay the government, or settle debts.

But lots and lots of things can serve those functions. My wife will serve me dinner every night in exchange for me taking out the garbage once a week. Obviously there is a store of value there. She will give me dinner five or six times before I have to do anything. We also agree that there is a price and that there is an exchange. Five or six dinners per garbage disposal.

But does me taking out the garbage make the garbage bag a medium of exchange? Obviously not.

The economic definition of money doesn't actually help much when it comes to telling us what money is.

The best way to think about money, I find, is to think about what money is not rather than what money is.

If money did not exist, we would be reduced to bartering for things we need and want. In other words, I could get someone to make me a t-shirt in exchange for me singing them a Miley Cyrus song. Or you, presumably being more talented than I, could fix someone's car in exchange for a pair of shoes.

Every thing that allows us to get away from this barter world is money.

To put it in a positive way, money is something that can hold its value over time (at least a day or so), whose value can be easily measured against things that we may need or want that are for sale, and that most people we want to transact with will accept.

Throughout history many different things have been money. Human beings have used barley, peppercorns, glass, gold, silver and even pieces of paper with no apparent value as money.

But if you think about it, money by itself is not actually all that interesting. Money is only interesting when it is used in human interactions. No one really cares what the value of a piece of gold buried under a pile of rocks is. That gold is only valuable if you are trying to use it to get something else.

It is when human beings become involved that money becomes interesting. This makes sense. Money, after all, is a human invention. In fact, it is not just a human invention. Modern money is decidedly an American invention.

To understand how money works and how the exchange of money, or payments, work we have to understand the history of payments in the United States.

That is the aim of this book; to give a cursory review of how we got to where we got.

We'll start with some basic assumptions about money. We won't go too far back. There will be no discussion in this book about invention of money. For a fascinating history of money, read *The Ascent of Money: A Financial History of the World* by Niall Ferguson.

The focus of this book will be the modern history of money and how people pay for things. We will start at a time when gold and silver coins were the most broadly accepted forms of payment. We'll start there because for much of the history of money before gold and silver came into play, humanity was at a loss trying to figure out how to find something that served the three functions of money best. We'll focus on the United States because virtually every innovation since humanity figured out that gold and silver were probably better forms of money than barley and rice (for one, they could not be eaten by rodents and were more easily transported) has had its footing in the United States.

A final note. This is not an academic work. Its goal isn't to tell the reader everything the reader should know about money. The goal is much simpler. The aim is to tell the entertaining history of payments in the United States so as to demystify why things work the way they do.

Okay. You've been adequately warned. If you keep reading, you have no one to blame but yourself.

1 BILLS AND CASH

The modern history of money in the world is inextricably linked with the fact that for centuries the people of Massachusetts seem to have been unable to get their state's government in order.

For much of its early history and especially in the late 17th century, the government of Massachusetts did not collect enough in taxes to fund its extravagant spending plans. To make up for this shortfall, the government of Massachusetts would fund its activities by launching plunder expeditions against Canada.

Being short on many things, including gold coins, armies from Massachusetts would head north to Quebec to invade and plunder treasures from the rich but poorly defended French territory. Of course, since it was short on money, Massachusetts did not have the funds necessary to pay soldiers up front for this campaigns. Those governing Massachusetts would simply assume that their expeditions to plunder Quebec would be successful and that he soldiers could be paid once the army returned to Boston and sold its booty.

Year after year, this was a good assumption. In October 1690, however, the Canadians were ready for war. They had a new leader who had grown tired of losing battles. Given the chance to surrender, to lose some money and to live to fight another day, Governor-General Louis de Buade de Frontenac said to the invading Massachusetts army that his only response to the offer of surrender would be by "the mouth of my cannons."

What was supposed to be a short plunder campaign turned into a long battle - a battle for which the invading army from New England was ill prepared. After weeks of futile battles, in late October 1690, the Massachusetts army waved the white flag and retreated in a state of panic leaving many valuable field guns on the battlefield in a rush back to Boston.

A few weeks later, the army arrived back in Boston with no booty but with thousands of pounds in debt to the returning soldiers whose salary had not yet been paid.

Unfortunately, Massachusetts had no money. It had no reserve of gold and no silver coins. The whole purpose of these plunder campaigns to Quebec was to fill the treasury in Boston with gold and silver. It seems that no one had considered what might happen should one of these campaigns not end with a surplus of gold and silver coin.

In desperation, the government of Massachusetts turned to Boston merchants as a source of 3,000 pounds in gold coins the government needed to borrow to pay the soldiers; but Massachusetts had a history of not paying its bills and Boston merchants, more shrewd than patriotic, were unwilling to lend the government any money.

In a crunch and facing a group of ornery, well-armed soldiers, the government of Massachusetts did something that no government had ever done before.

In December 1690, right before Christmas, the government of Massachusetts invented paper currency.

Instead of turning to merchants and bankers from other colonies, knowing that the answer from all of them was likely no, Massachusetts simply turned on its printers and printed pieces of paper that it claimed were worth 7,000 pounds.

Knowing that soldiers might question the value of paper, Massachusetts made two promises. First, it promised that the paper notes would be exchanged for gold or silver within a couple of years. Second, it promised that it would never print any paper money ever again.

Of course, as we now know, Massachusetts kept neither of these promises. It printed more money within weeks and it did not settle the notes handed out to the soldiers for decades.

The Massachusetts government's penchant for paper alchemy caused some concern in the old colony. The whole idea behind the paper currency had been a promise that the government would be able to exchange it for gold at some point. If Massachusetts kept printing more and more money, everyone was relatively certain that it would never have the gold reserve needed to pay off these paper notes.

Seeing this, the soldiers who were holding this paper currency began selling them on the open market to whoever was willing to exchange them for gold right away. As more and more holders of paper money sold their money in exchange for gold, the value of the paper fell more and more.

Within a year the value of the world's first fiat currency had fallen by nearly 50%.

Seeing this devaluation, Massachusetts had two options. It could have stopped printing money or it could have brought in a law requiring that the paper money be the official legal money of the colony and not subject to devaluation.

Massachusetts, once again facing a massive budget shortfall and lack of coins, chose the latter. It continued printing massive amounts of paper money - 500,000 pounds of it in one month in 1691. It also brought in a law that anyone not accepting the paper money at par with gold or silver would be jailed and have all of his or her property confiscated by the government.

Seeing Massachusetts' almost unending ability to fund its expenses through printing of money, other colonies quickly followed suit.

As other colonies began printing money, Massachusetts inflation got worse. It could no longer rely on its relatively worthless currency to be exchanged for gold and silver in Rhode Island or Connecticut. For example, in 1740 the value of Massachusetts printed money fell by 46%. In 1747, it fell by 46%. By 1750, the par value of Massachusetts money had collapsed by more than 90%.

The currency devaluation between 1690 and 1750 had become such a problem that it ultimately required the Parliament in London to intervene directly in Massachusetts' monetary policy. The colonial legislature in Massachusetts passed a law, in 1749, effectively banning its own paper currency. It ordered that all paper currency outstanding to be returned by March 31, 1750 and exchange for gold sent by His Majesty King George's treasury to Massachusetts.

Additionally, Massachusetts passed a law making it a criminal offence to bring any paper money from its neighboring colonies, New Hampshire, Rhode Island, and Connecticut into Massachusetts.

This ban on use of paper currency had the desired effect in Massachusetts. To the delight of merchants and consumers, by April 1, 1750, virtually all paper money had disappeared from Massachusetts. While the disappearance of paper money from the colony caused a shortage of coins and other means of exchange, at least the spiraling Massachusetts hyperinflation had been stopped.

To fight the shortage of coins, a few months after the retirement of its now worthless currency, Massachusetts introduced a new kind of paper currency. This time, the paper currency was not simply backed by a promise that it would eventually be exchanged for gold at some future date - it was a treasury note that differed from money in three very important ways.

First, unlike the earlier paper currency, these notes were not legal tender. They could not be used to repay debts and no merchant was obligated to accept them as a form of payment. Second, while they were outstanding, they earned interest to be paid by the government of

Massachusetts. Third, they could be converted on demand into gold or silver coins.

These three features meant that the government of Massachusetts could not simply print endless amounts of money as it had before.

Having seen the experience in Massachusetts, in 1751 the Parliament in London on the advice of King George forbid all colonies in New England from printing paper money.

By 1752, the flood of paper money into the United States had turned into a trickle - but the dam was about to burst with the Revolutionary War in 1775.

As Massachusetts had previously learned from its repeated attempts to invade Canada, and as the Founding Fathers of the United States would soon learn, wars - especially against the British empire - cost an obscene amount of money.

Soldiers, even volunteers, must be fed. They must be armed. They must be housed. To pay for these expenses, the newly minted United States began issuing its own paper currency. This currency, called a Continental, would be issued for a limited time and in a limited amount, the new United States government promised. Within 7 years, the people were told, this currency would be retired using the taxes that would be levied by the victorious states of the new country.

Of course, as had been the case in Massachusetts almost a century earlier, the new Congress did not abide by its promise to limit the printing. Instead, the US Congress authorized the printing of an almost unlimited amount of the Continental paper currency.

Because of this massive influx of new money, backed by virtually nothing other than a promise, the value of the Continental fell almost immediately after its introduction. A year after its introduction, the Continental was worth 25% less than it had been upon introduction.

Seeing this decline, King George delighted in the failure of the new currency. Correctly assuming that the United States could be harmed if its money supply was attacked, British forces in the United States began creating counterfeit currency as a way of undermining the public's trust in the new US currency, and as an extension, the new country itself.

The proliferation of counterfeit bills and the fact that Congress had increased the total money supply in the United States by nearly 20-fold in 4 years caused the value of the Continental to collapse. By 1780, Continentals had one-fortieth of the value that they had upon issue. In fact, the American idiom that something is "not worth a continental" started out as a way to mock the new US currency.

Unsurprisingly, in 1780 the production of the Continental was discontinued. During this civil war period, several states had also began printing money that had become virtually worthless by the end of the war.

This meant that by the time the Founding Fathers of the United States gathered in Philadelphia on May 25, 1787, the United States federal and state governments had experienced and failed at creating and maintaining at least a dozen different forms of paper money. Some, like Maryland's "indented bills" were actually paper backed by stock in the Bank of England. Others, like those in Pennsylvania favored by Benjamin Franklin, were "coined land" which was simply a paper currency backed by real estate. Interestingly, Franklin, as a businessman, had helped design and print the failed paper money in most of the early colonies. He was personally responsible for the design of the currencies of New Jersey, Pennsylvania and Delaware.

The Coinage Clause

It was against this backdrop that James Madison was tasked with drafting of the US constitution. Madison a representative from Virginia, was particularly well-versed with the history of paper currencies. Virginia's paper currency had the dishonor of being one of the weakest and most devalued currencies of the new world.

Madison's view of paper currencies and competing currencies was firmly set out by him in Federalist Papers No. 42 where he wrote that

> "All that need be remarked on the power to coin money, regulate the value thereof, and of foreign coin, is, that by providing for this last case, the Constitution has supplied a material omission in the articles of Confederation. The authority of the existing Congress is restrained to the regulation of coin struck by their own authority, or that of the respective States. It must be seen at once that the proposed uniformity in the value of the current coin might be destroyed by subjecting that of foreign coin to the different regulations of the different States. . . . The regulation of weights and measures is transferred from the articles of

Confederation, and is founded on like considerations with the preceding power of regulating coin."

Some historians have suggested that Madison was not just weary of states issuing paper money, he was also opposed to Congress having the power to issue paper money going as far as saying that he would only approve of Congress having the power to issue paper money if it were not considered legal tender in the United States.

After the initial discussions about currency during the constitutional conventions, the constitutional wording in an early draft giving Congress power over money in the United States (including deletions) looked like this:

"To ~~regulate~~ The exclusive right of coining money ~~Paper prohibit~~ no State to be perd. in future to emit Paper Bills of Credit witht. the App: of the Natl. Legisle nor to make any ~~Article~~ Thing but Specie a Tender in paymt of debts."

From reading this initial draft and the text of the debates that took place during the conventions, it is relatively clear that at least some of the drafters of the US constitution were so shocked by the inflationary effects of paper currency printed by the states that they wanted to ensure that a) no state would ever be allowed to have a say over monetary policy ever again and b) no paper money ever be issued in the United States.

During the debates that followed, however, the majority of the convention participants opposed the express prohibition on Congress printing paper currency. Thus the final version of the US constitution, in Article 1 Section 8, giving the power to control US currency to Congress reads that [Congress shall have power] "To coin Money, regulate the Value thereof, and of foreign Coin."

In case this article was not clear, the US Founding Fathers added Article 1 Section 10 to the US Constitution the relevant part of which reads "No state shall ... coin Money, emit Bills of Credit; make any Thing but gold and silver Coin a Tender in Payment of Debts."

Having seen the failure of paper money issued in mass by various states, the Founding Fathers had had enough. Federal government was going to step in, as King George had once, to save the day.

US Gold & Silver Coins

Given the testy relations with England and the significant trade volume with Spanish colonies, the Spanish silver dollar was the most prominent coin in use in the US in the lead up to and after US independence.

Congress, having been given the power to coin money, was generally expected to name the dollar as the basic currency of the United States. And Congress did not disappoint. Congress disappointing the American people did not become a fact of life until much later in America's history.

In 1792, upon the recommendation of Secretary of Treasury Alexander Hamilton, Congress passed, and President Washington signed, the Coinage Act of 1792.

The new law established the US dollar as a gold, silver, or copper coin with specific weights for each. The most common coins issued under the law were the silver one dollar coins, the $10 gold eagle coins, the $5 golden half-eagles and the $2.50 gold quarter-eagles.

To avoid having a shortage of money, in 1793, Congress also passed a law stating that all foreign coins in the United States would also be legal tender. This would mean that even after the introduction of the US dollar, Spanish dollar coins were by far the most popular currency in the United States. This fact bothered many Americans who viewed it as their patriotic duty to promote a US dollar.

In 1797, President John Adams put forward a proposal to terminate the legal tender of all foreign currencies. This plan, however, was rebuffed since it was believed that it would actually lead to a shortage of currency since the US mint was incapable of producing enough US dollar coins.

In fact, US coins were so infrequently used that in late 1790s a US congressman told the House of Representatives that "it was as difficult to find a gold as it was a flying eagle." It was not until 1857, when the use of coins had generally decreased, that Congress passed the Coinage Act of 1857 and finally ended the life of the Spanish dollar as a legal tender in the United States.

Free Banking

Between 1792 and the start of US Civil War in 1861, much of the innovation in currency was done by private banks issuing private bank notes that were traded as currency. These bank notes would allow depositors to deposit their gold and silver coins with the bank and carry around with them paper money that was broadly accepted by merchants in the region who knew the bank's reputation. Like the second generation paper notes from

Massachusetts, these bank notes could be converted into gold or silver on demand by simply showing up at the bank's office.

One such bank was the First National Bank of the United States which issued paper currency. While the First Bank of the United State of the United States was chartered by the US government and had the US government as a shareholder, its currency was not official legal tender. In fact, its currency had no more official a position than the currency of dozens of other privately held banks, chartered by various states, that opened shop. Even after the collapse of the First Bank of the United States in in 1811, many such private banks thrived.

In the next 50 years, in addition to the government owned banks, nearly 1,000 private banks opened up in the United States almost always serving a special group of merchants.

Many of these banks were not really banks as much as they were lending arms of a local guild. They were usually located inside a merchant's shop and allowed companies dealing with the merchant to buy or sell goods on credit. Many of them, however, also issued paper currency backed by their deposits of gold and silver. Some of them even issued more currency than they had gold or silver on reserve in order to expand the volume of paper currency in the economy. These banks assumed, as banks do today, that it would be very rare that 100% of all their notes would come due for gold or silver at the same time. Therefore, they could comfortably issue notes in excess of the amount of gold and silver they had on deposit.

During this so-called "free banking" period, the United States was filled with hundreds of different currencies all with different values and different reliability. In fact, money brokers would publish books with some frequency including a list of all banks and the value of their currency compared to gold or silver.

This created massive fraud and inflation. A merchant would have to carry in his shop a book so that he would know whether the bank whose name was printed on a piece of paper would exist by the time the merchant tried to redeem the bill for gold. This system, obviously, could not last for long. It didn't.

Greenbacks

To meet the government's financial needs during the Civil War, President Abraham Lincoln borrowed significant amounts of money. In order to pay for this debt and to avoid having hundreds of different types of currencies in the country, Congress passed the Legal Tender Act of 1862.

The new law allowed the issuance of printed money, known as "Greenbacks" because green ink was used on the back of the paper currency. These greenbacks were the official currency of the United States and legal tender. They would be issued and accepted instead of and alongside of gold and silver coins.

A year later, Congress passed the National Banking Act to create a single national currency. This Act placed a very high tax on any currency that was not the national currency and thus, in effect, banned private bank currencies. No one would want to buy a drink for $1 in greenbacks but $10 in some bank's private note. Had it been successful, this law could have made the greenback the national currency of the United States replacing gold and silver dollar coins.

Unfortunately for the greenback, however, California and Oregon refused to accept greenback as currency. Flushed with gold due to the gold rush, merchants and governments in the Western states refused to accept greenbacks. So even despite a national currency law, greenbacks could not become the national currency.

Outside California and Oregon, greenback had other issues. Just like the early currency of Massachusetts, greenbacks were not on demand notes. They could not be easily converted to gold, so their value depended on the American population's trust in their government's finances.

As the civil war went on, based on the turn of each battle and the money required to fight it, the merchants in the United States had less and less reason to trust the central government's ability to finance itself. Thus in their first full year in circulation, in 1862, the value of greenback against gold fell by nearly 29%. Three months later, in Spring 1863, the value of greenback against gold had fell by another 30% or so. The currency kept losings its value and at its lowest point, in July 1864 as confederate General Jubal Early led his forces within five miles of Washington, D.C., to buy something that would've cost $100 in gold you would have had to pay $258 in greenbacks.

Because of these troubles, massive debt incurred during the war, and inflationary pressure on greenbacks, the US federal government stopped printing greenbacks in late 1865 and by 1879 greenbacks were completely out of circulation. Interestingly, greenbacks were topic of such political debate that they gave rise to a political party. In the 1878 elections, the Greenback-Labor Party elected 14 members of Congress. Even in as late as 2015, the old greenback had fans. A petition requesting that President Obama restate the greenback as the official currency of the United States received 14 signatures. How the mighty fall.

Redemption of Gold

With the death of the greenback obvious in 1866, Congress passed the Contraction Act allowing the greenbacks to be converted into gold by the US Treasury.

Three years later, Congress passed the Public Credit Act of 1869. This law allowed the US government to pay back all civil war debt back in gold. While this law did not actually reestablish gold as the official currency of the United States, it created a political environment in which gold could be re-established as currency. It was not until 1875, when Congress passed the Specie Payment Resumption Act of 1875 (better known simply as the Resumption Act), that silver and gold once again became the national currency of the United States - though silver was practically never used and silver dollars were never minted after 1875.

In 1877, two years after the Resumption Act, Congress passed a law making the Bureau of Engraving and Printing, which had been founded in 1862 to print greenbacks, the exclusive supplier of U.S. currency. From then until today, the Bureau of Engraving and Printing has been the exclusive printer of money in the United States.

Federal Reserve

By 1900, for the first time since its founding, the United States had a single currency (the US dollar), backed by a single asset (gold), and printed at a single place (the Bureau of Engraving and Printing); but this did not mean that the United States was done making significant changes to US currency.

While the federal government had finally instituted a national banking system and a US currency, it still didn't have much influence over how many notes were floating around the US economy. The number of notes produced was still influenced by the banks. The Treasury Department, which housed the Bureau of Engraving and Printing, merely printed the currency. It did not determine its supply which was still governed by the amount of reserves held by private banks.

The overwhelming power of private banks over currency created problems through the late 1890s and early 1900s. The combination of bank control over the flow of US currency and fractional reserves, i.e. the ability of a bank to create more money than it has deposits or gold on hand, meant that the failure of one bank often created a so called panic. A panic could occur if a bank, for example, had only $100,000 in gold in its vault but had accepted as deposits and obligations $500,000. This bank would be fine since it is unlikely that more than 1 in 5 of its customers would demand all their money on a given day. However, if the customers of a bank believed that the bank was the on the verge of bankruptcy, then all of them would rush to the bank and create a "panic" demanding their money.

The most famous of these panics occurred in 1907. Over the course of three weeks in October 1907, the New York Stock Exchange lost 50% of its value. This led to a deep recession that caused the failure of several banks and bankruptcies of many prominent businesses.

Oddly enough, the Panic of 1907, which started in New York was actually caused by an event the year earlier in San Francisco.

At 5 am on April 18, 1906, a great earthquake leveled San Francisco. The earthquake also caused a fire that destroyed nearly every building in San Francisco. Particularly hard hit were all the banks in the city because they were all located at the epicenter of the fire.

None of the banks could open up their doors and none could get into their vaults to see whether there was anything left of their gold and currency deposits. Wells Fargo's president, in order to avoid a run on his bank sent out a telegram to all depositors "Building destroyed. Vaults intact. Credit Unaffected". Of course, he was only sure of the first sentence. There was no way for him to know if the vault was in fact intact or if all his credit had disappeared.

In the aftermath of the fire, San Francisco's two largest banks, Wells Fargo and Bank of Italy (which would go on to become Bank of America), began underwriting loans well above their gold reserves in order to rebuild the city.

This caused a great stress on the American money supply. Virtually all the excess money from all over the country was being sucked into San Francisco. This meant that there was little money that banks could lend to each other for much of the following year.

This would not have been cause for much concern, except that on October 16, 1907 two relatively large stock speculators in New York went bankrupt. Months of trouble in the stock market meant that these two brokers no longer had the money to cover their losses.

Unfortunately for the banking world, these two stockbrokers were also connected with a handful of banks in New York and their well-publicized bankruptcy caused depositors at these banks to run to the branches asking for their money.

Typically some other bank would have lent these troubled banks money, but so much money had gone to San Francisco that there was less than usual left in New York. The money left was not enough to cover the deposits at many banks.

In a span of a few days, nearly a dozen prominent banks were forced to close their doors. The crisis only ended when J.P. Morgan personally stepped in to lend money to many of the banks to end the bank failures.

In response to the Panic of 1907 and in order to get a better control over the flow of money in the country, in 1913, Congress passed the Federal Reserve Act. With this law, Congress gave the Federal Reserve, not private banks, the power to set the monetary policy of the United States; and the Federal Reserve, not the private banks, now had the power to lend as much money as it could print to banks to avoid bank failures.

With the exception of the end of the gold standard (the discussion of which is well beyond the scope of this book), the United States has had the same basic structure when it comes to currency since the creation of the Federal Reserve.

2 CHECKS IN AMERICA

Unlike government backed paper currency, checks are not a completely American invention.

It is very likely that checks existed in one form or another during the reign of the Roman empire since the idea of checks appears in early Latin poetry. Ovid, who died in 17 AD, wrote about a day when a rich man is trying to impress his wife.

> But when she has her purchase in her eye,
> She hugs thee close, and kisses thee to buy;
> "Tis what I want, and 'tis a pen'orth too;
> In many years I will not trouble you."
> If you complain you have no ready coin,
> No matter, 'tis but writing of a line;
> A little bill, not to be paid at sight:
> "Now curse the time when thou wert taught to write."

While they were likely invented in ancient Rome, checks

became popular in Holland, where, in the 1500s, merchants and international shippers would deposit their gold and silver coins with a counterparty in exchange for a cashier's note. This way, the gold and the silver would not have to make a long trek home and become hunted bounty for pirates.

Between the early 1500s and the late 1600s, not much changed in the world of checking. Checks were used with some frequency among international shippers and some merchants, but the general public and even most merchants looked at checks with suspicion.

Boston in 1681

That all changed in Boston in 1681. Yes. Boston, again.

Boston, in the early 1600's, was an odd town. It was part of the new world, yet desperately trying to be anything but new. It was ruled by the most religious puritans to land in the new world. It wanted a government, but refused to pay for it. It wanted to conquer Canada, but refused to commit to an all out assault.

By 1681, a decade before the ill-fated attack on Canada which led to the rise of government backed currency, Boston had started modernizing and had a growing business population. The city reversed a 20-year old ban on celebrating Christmas, put in place originally to stop the dancing associated with the holiday, and began building itself as a center of both commerce and religion.

It was this growth in Boston that caused a shortage of currency. People wanted to buy and sell things—but they didn't have enough gold and silver coins.

To remedy this situation, in September 1681 a group of Boston businessmen got together and crated The Fund at Boston in New England. These businessmen mortgaged their land to this Fund, received credits for the value of the land and then drew checks against this fund to buy and sell things.

As The Fund at Boston in New England grew in popularity, other similar funds were started in other cities and towns in the United States.

These funds bought checks from local merchants without charging any fees; local checks, therefore, were cleared at par. In other words the funds paid the check holder the full amount of the check.

The funds, however, did charge a fee for checks that were mailed to them from out of town for settlement. This fee originally was meant to cover the costs of sending gold coins, frequently via horse carriage, to the fund or the bank that had received the check from one of its customers.

As US merchants began to travel more and more, these out of town check fees became more and more common.

To gain a competitive edge in the local market and to receive more business from local merchants, many local banks developed a network of relationships with out-of-town banks. These networks would allow banks to cash checks between each other without any fees.

Frequently meeting in local restaurants or train stations, employees from these banks would simply batch a week's worth of checks and exchange them at pre-set meeting destinations, so-called clearing houses. These clearing houses were frequently placed close to train stations so that travel by rail would be easier for those making the trips every week. (Interestingly, to this day in an homage to the early days the term "payment rails" is used to refer to a system over which payments can be settled.)

At the meetings in the clearing houses, the banks would simply exchange checks and settle the difference in gold coin or letters of credit.

Under this ad hoc system, banks began sending checks to their network partners rather than the original bank. For example, if Bank A in Boston had a relationship with Bank B in Philadelphia, and was presented with a check from the Bank C in Philadelphia, Bank A would send the check to Bank B , and an employee from Bank B would then simply physically walk up to a branch of Bank C in Philadelphia and clear the check at par.

As these networks became more complicated, the routing of checks became more complicated as well. Checks would frequently travel hundreds of miles more than they needed to in order to be cleared at par.

While banks reduced the fees they paid using this clearance method, they did not reduce the fees they charged to their customers. This meant that starting in the 1700s, banks were making a significant amount of money from check interchange.

This created some very odd incentives for banks. Obviously reducing the cost of clearance led to an increase in time of settlement. A check that had to exchange hands 10 or 12 times would likely land in an account weeks after it was written. This meant that by the time the check was ultimately settled, the customer might no longer have sufficient funds in their account.

In one example, a check drawn from a Sag Harbor, New York bank travelled more than 1,200 miles through nearly ten cities before being deposited in Hoboken, New Jersey, which is less than 100 miles away from Sag Harbor.

In another example, a check deposited in an Alabama bank that was written from a bank merely a few city blocks away was routed nearly 2,500 miles, through Jacksonville and Philadelphia before returning to Alabama a week later.

In addition to increasing the credit risk, this system increased the risk of error. A check traveling 2000 miles might be lost, might be recorded incorrectly, or might be stolen by bandits along the way—a non-trivial risk in those days.

Spike in Popularity

For much of the two centuries between 1681 and the Civil War in 1861, checks lagged in usage behind government backed currency and private bank currency (the type that were taxed out of existence by the National Bank Act in 1870s).

By the 1850s, however, as private banks flourished and as free banks spread across the United States, checks became more and more popular. By the end of the Civil War, given all the trouble with the devaluation of greenbacks and shortage of gold and silver, checks were the most popular method of payment in the United States. This growth, incidentally, did not slow down until the late

1990s.

By the early 1940s, Americans were writing nearly four billion checks each year. That means that each American was writing on average a check every 11 days. By the 1950s, Americans were writing nearly eight billion checks each year. This works out to each American writing at least one check every week.

By 1979, nearly 90% of all payments in the United States were made by check. Americans wrote checks for nearly every purchase - writing a total of 33 billion checks in 1979. That's one check written every other day by each man, woman and child in the United States.

Interestingly, as the usage of checks in every day life grew the shape and the design of checks did not change much. The only major difference between a check written in 1860 and a check written in 1960 would have been the introduction of the magnetic ink character recognition code (MICR Code) at the bottom of the check in 1959.

Federal Reserve to the Rescue - Again

The system developed in 1681 for clearing a few dozen checks was collapsing by the late 1800s.

As checks became more popular and more fees were incurred, the US merchant population began lobbying Congress to fix what the merchants considered a banking racket.

The merchants, and some banks, began lobbying Congress to create a central bank. The US. Congress was skeptical. Two previous efforts to create a central bank (in 1791 and in 1816) had not ended well. Thomas Jefferson and Andrew Jackson had both spent a significant part of their political lives opposing such banks, arguing that they were unconstitutional and unnecessary.

But in 1913, spurred by the Panic of 1907 as discussed in the previous chapter, Congress finally relented and passed the Federal Reserve Act, giving the new Federal Reserve Board the specific task of getting rid of expensive check fees.

The Federal Reserve took up this task with gusto, and began to force—frequently by threat of forcing a bank into effective insolvency—an at-par check clearance system on US banks. By 1920, nearly 20,000 banks in the United States had signed up for the "voluntary" at-par clearance system. A few hold-outs sued the Federal Reserve. In the famous Am. Bank & Trust Co. v. Fed. Res. Bank of Atlanta case, the Supreme Court ruled in favor of the bank, and against the Federal Reserve.

The Supreme Court ruled that the Federal Reserve had been acting unconstitutionally and illegally by forcing banks to join its at-par clearance system.

> "Congress did not in terms confer upon the Federal Reserve Board or the federal reserve banks a duty to establish universal par clearance and collection of checks; and there is nothing in the original act or in any amendment from which such duty to compel its adoption may be inferred."

Immediately after this decision, the number of banks charging check interchange went up. In the long run, however, the damage had been done. So many merchants had found banks willing to clear their transactions at par that the remaining banks wanting to charge interchange gave up their fight and waived their fees as well.

3 AUTOMATED CLEARING HOUSE

As checks grew in popularity, more and more employees began requesting that their employers pay them in check rather than cash.

By the late 1950s, virtually every single salaried employee in the United States was being paid by check. Every two weeks, payroll teams across America would gather their records and begin the process of paying their employees. Once these checks were written, they were handed to the employees, many of whom would immediately drive to the nearest bank to deposit their salary into their bank account.

This traffic of payroll clerks writing checks, managers signing them and employees depositing them became particularly problematic in California where thanks to intense expansion of Bank of America the percentage of employees with bank accounts was higher than elsewhere in the country.

SCOPE

The increased travel to their branches and the delays associated with writing and depositing checks every two weeks for the exact same amount drove many bankers in San Francisco to the edge. Thus, more out of frustration than anything else, in 1968 a group of San Francisco bankers invited some Los Angeles bankers to form the Special Committee on Paperless Entries (SCOPE).

The people running SCOPE didn't have any great national plans. They didn't want to form a new method of payment. They just wanted to find a way to free their bank clerks from the drudgery of having to spend hours upon hours every two weeks reviewing and depositing paychecks.

This task became more difficult during Christmas season. A New Jersey banker, from this period, claimed once in an interview that during the Christmas season the paperwork required to settle all transactions, including all the checks, would reach the ceiling of the bank's main branch and that it would take the bank's employees up to four months to clear such transactions. During this four month period, the bank would not know whether it had been defrauded or whether it had cashed a bad check.

The task of SCOPE, therefore, while a thankless one was a necessary one. Left with the processes from the 1960s, banks would not be able to fit all the paper required to track all transactions in the back offices of their branches by the 1980s.

The amount of paper piling up in bank offices was especially problematic in California. By 1968, many Californians were using the then popular BankAmericard cards (covered in a later chapter) for their purchases and these transactions would need to be settled and paid for by many of the same clerks that were responsible for maintaining the checking system for many banks.

In order to deal with the increasing flow of transactions from all the checks being written, SCOPE used a relatively recent innovation from the world of checks.

Starting in 1959, banks had begun printing magnetic ink character recognition codes, or MICR codes, at the bottom of their checks. This ink was meant to be used in conjunction with the relatively new optical character recognition, or OCR, technology to lessen the work of manually looking up and writing account information on the back of checks so they could be proceed.

Against this backdrop, starting in 1968, the SCOPE committee started to solve the problem at hand. Early on the committee decided that its goal was to create an exchange called "Automatic Payments and Deposit Exchange" to enable "preauthorized paperless entry" of transactions.

As they navigated the legalities, the lawyers in the room advised the group to not call their final organization an exchange but a clearing house. Thus, with the help of the Federal Reserve of San Francisco, SCOPE formed the California Automated Clearing House Network (CACH).

The system called on the member banks to send CACH two transmissions on a daily basis either on magnetic tapes or punch card, though preferably magnetic tape. The first transmission involved all the debit transactions that a bank wished to originate – in effect pulling funds from another bank. The second transmission involved all the credit transactions. Banks were forbidden from sending their "on us" transactions, transactions where the debit and the credit accounts are held at the same bank, to CACH.

One may ask, why are banks required to send two separate transmissions to the clearing house? This is an odd feature of the Automated Clearing House ("ACH") system that persists to this day.

The reasons were simple.

First, the debit and the credit features of the system were built on two fundamentally different procedures. A debit transfer was very similar to a check clearing process. All that changed was the lack of a paper check. The credit transfer, however, was built on top of the already existing pre-authorized payroll deposit system where some employers required that their employees open up bank accounts at the employer's bank in order to facilitate payroll. These two systems were fundamentally different systems within banks.

Second, and more practically, the magnetic tapes available in 1968 did not have enough storage for both outgoing and incoming transactions. This meant that even if banks were willing to change their internal procedures, they could not find storage tapes with enough capacity for their needs.

For comparison, the most sophisticated magnetic drum

memory in the late 1950s had a capacity of around 10 Kilobytes. A Kilobyte is 1,024 Bytes. A Kilobyte can hold about 2 paragraphs of text. A Gigabyte is 1,073,741,824 Bytes or 1,048,576 Kilobytes. A Gigabyte can hold every song ever recorded by Miley Cyrus. It can hold Party In The USA about 256 times over. The least expensive iPhone 7 in 2017 has a capacity of 32 Gigabytes.

Another challenge facing SCOPE in 1968 was the fact that what its ultimate goal had recently been made illegal.

For over 100 years, the law governing payments of checks in the United States was the egotiable Instruments Law of 1896. It had very broad structures around what was allowed and what wasn't, but it gave banks and clearing houses a great deal of flexibility.

In 1951, however, the Negotiable Instruments Law was replaced by the Uniform Commercial Code. The old rules were modified and became Article 3 within the Uniform Commercial Code, called "Negotiable Instruments". The rest of the old rules were included in Article 4 of the new Uniform Commercial Code called "Bank Deposits and Collections".

Under the new rules, a check was a negotiable instruments and thus covered by Article 3; but Article 4 governed the specific rules that banks must abide by when handling checks.

Article 3, among other things, required that a negotiable instrument contain a signature and a promise to pay. It is difficult to imagine how a magnetic tape or a punch card could contain either a signature or a promise to pay. In fact, the file system envisioned by SCOPE would only contain account numbers and debit or credit amounts.

This meant that any law that could permit SCOPE to do what it wanted to do must be based either on Article 4 or a sophisticated contract between all the banks specifically nullifying provisions of the Uniform Commercial Code. It is easy to imagine how negotiating such a contract would be difficult and expensive.

Luckily for SCOPE, Article 4 did allow for payments of "any instrument for the payment of money even though it is not negotiable." However, even here the banks were not clear.

Article 4 clearly governed rules of an "instrument"; and the term instrument is defined within the Uniform Commercial Code as a "writing".

SCOPE's legal advisors brazenly argued that since a writing means "an intentional reduction to tangible form" then holes in a punch card or data on a magnetic tape would also constitute a "writing". No one apparently asked how 1s and 0s stored on a digital tape themselves were "tangible". Fewer people seemed to argue that a hole is not something tangible but by definition the lack of something tangible.

To make the legal case murkier, Article 4 imposed on the banks to use reasonable care to discover "unauthorized signature or any alternation of an item" and to send to the customer "a statement of account accompanied by items paid in good faith."

Obviously, under SCOPE's plan the bank could not take reasonable care to review unauthorized signatures on every debit and credit entry. SCOPE's lawyers reasoned that the bank could review the signature on the original instruction for the repeat transactions and that this would be enough despite the fact that court cases had leaned towards interpreting the law to mean that this duty applied to every transaction.

The lawyers also argued that the simply printing what was on the magnetic tape and attaching it to the monthly statement would be enough to comply with the "statement" requirement of Article 4. This is peculiar, of course, since the information on the magnetic tape and the information on the statement would be drawn from the exact same source. They would not allow the customer to see any mistakes with the underlying instructions.

Despite the legal objections, SCOPE's lawyers consented to its plans. The pain felt by California banks from paper checks piling up in their branches was too strong to be stopped by mere legalities that would take years to litigate through the courts.

The same thing, however, could not be said about the California labor laws. Unlike the Uniform Commercial Code, California labor laws are not optional. Even if the banks wanted to spend years negotiating contracts between themselves, they could not opt out of California labor laws. More importantly, there was no ambiguity in California's labor laws. They required, in black and white, that no company "shall issue in payment of wages due ... any order, check, draft, note ... , unless it is negotiable and payable in cash, on demand."

Virtually none of these conditions were met by the system envisions by SCOPE. The payments would not be "negotiable" since they clearly did not meet requirements set out in Article 3 of Uniform Commercial Code. The payments would not be in payable in cash or on demand. A payment made on Monday would show up in the customer's bank account later in the week and even then it may not be payable in cash since the customer may have other obligations to the bank. The money would simply be added on top of the customer's existing balance and if that balance were negative the payment would be reduced.

This meant that before launching any system the banks would need to change California law. After much lobbying and after making it clear that customers would not be charged any fees for receiving payments under the system envisioned by SCOPE, California banks convinced the California legislature to change California law to make it clear that payments made electronically under the system envisioned by SCOPE were an acceptable method of payment of wages in California so long as the employees receiving the payment voluntarily opted into such a system.

Thus, after four long years of work, in the late afternoon of October 13, 1972, the world's first paperless transaction was completed when magnetic tapes containing information from a few banks arrived in the San Francisco federal reserve building.

By January 1973, less than three months after the first automated clearance between the banks, nearly every dollar deposited in California was held by a bank that was a member of CACH.

CACH was very clear, and narrow, in its mandate. It was designed to "replace checks as a mechanism for the making of mortgage, insurance, utility and other regularly recurring payments by consumers, as well as for the making of wage, dividend and other recurring payments to consumers."

The system, in other words, was not designed to handle one-time transactions. It also was not designed to handle transactions that occurred on different dates.

The original CACH process required that a depositor, i.e. the person sending money, sign a document laying out the exact amount of a recurring transaction and the date on which it was to be made. If a customer wanted to send $8 a month to the utility company and $200 a month to pay his or her mortgage, the customer had to provide two different documents. Each document would instruct the bank to make these recurring payments and it would be valid until the consumer went into a branch to revoke the instructions.

Perhaps because of these limitations, CACH volume grew slowly. By early 1973, CACH proponents were predicting that by 1976 CACH or a system like it would replace 35% of all payroll checks and almost 10% of all checks in the United States with a paperless system.

In fact, as it turned out, in 1976 only 100 million ACH transactions were processed in the United Sates. That same year, US banks processed over 25 billion checks.

Even this lower than expected volume, however, was very attractive to banks all over the United States. In conjunction with CACH, multiple other regional clearing houses were founded across the United Sates.

NACHA

In 1974, the National Automated Clearinghouse Association (NACHA) was formed as a non-profit association to merge CACH, the Georgia Automated

Clearing House Association, the Upper Midwest Automated Clearing House Association, and the New England Automated Clearing House.

By 1978, virtually every bank in the United Sates was a member of NACHA and thus able to exchange funds and clear transactions without the use of paper throughout the country.

While NACHA became the rule-making body for ACH payments in 1978, it never took over the responsibility of clearing actual payments. Banks must also employ a so-called ACH operator to receive and transmit ACH files. As of 2017, only two such operators exist: the Federal Reserve and the Clearing House.

To this day, ACH is perhaps the least understood method of payment in the United Sates. While the initial uptake for ACH transactions was not as high CACH would have liked, ACH transactions have ballooned since the 1990s.

In many ways, ACH has become the underlying system beneath all non-cash payments. In 2017, a consumer may pay for a transaction at the point of sale with a credit card, but that transaction is settled between the various banks and retailers using ACH. The consumer almost certainly pays his or her bill at the end of the month using ACH. The credit card processor almost certainly pays the retailer using ACH.

Starting in 2001, even many check transactions are converted to ACH transactions before being processed. In 2017, virtually all non-cash transactions in the United States that involve more than one bank end up being ACH transactions somewhere along the way.

In 2015, for example, there were 2.56 trillion dollars' worth of debit transactions, 3.16 worth of credit transactions, and 26.83 trillion dollars' worth of check transactions. That same year, the United States had 54.76 trillion dollars' worth of ACH debit transactions and 90.54 trillion of ACH credit transactions.

If the world of payments were an apple pie, the credit card and debit card transactions would be the slice of the pie that the dog gets to eat after you accidentally dropped it on the floor. ACH would be the slice that your slightly inebriated uncle would want to grab if you let him. When it comes to value (not number) of transactions, ACH is basically the main game in town.

Full disclosure: My company, Kash, has developed a proprietary system of payments called Direct Debit which uses ACH as the underlying method of payments.

Direct Debit's goals are simple. Direct Debit allows merchants to accept payments from retailers without having to pay expensive credit card and debit card fees and without having to worry about credit card and debit card fraud. For more, please visit www.kashpayments.com

4 CARDS

Like bills and checks, the history of credit cards starts in Massachusetts.

It is difficult to tell when the first payment cards came into use - the answer depends on what one means by a payment card.

What is not difficult, however, is to tell who first invented the idea of the credit card. That honor belongs not to a banker, but to a science fiction writer named Edward Bellamy.

Published in 1888, *Looking Backward: 2000–1887* was one of the first commercially successful science fiction books written in English. It was the third-largest bestseller of its time, coming right after *Ben-Hur* in the bestseller tables.

The book is the Marxist version of *Atlas Shrugged*. After its publications, it almost immediately created a political movement. In the United States, over 150 so-called

"Bellamy Clubs" were formed to promote the book's propaganda against the capitalist state. These clubs, like the book, promoted nationalization of private property and attempted to influence the politics of the late 19th century United States. Interestingly, the year Looking Backward was published in the same year that the Greenback Party (mentioned in Chapter 1) was dissolved.

Looking Backward: 2000–1887 is the story of a young Bostonian who finds himself having travelled through time from 1887 to 2000. Having left the cruelty of capitalistic society in the late 1800s, Julian West finds himself awake in a socialist utopia in the year 2000.

In the year 2000, one of the first things that Julian West does is get himself a "credit card" – from best we can tell, this was the first time this phrase was used in the English language. The credit card envisioned by Bellamy in 1887 feels shockingly real.

> "... a credit card issued him with which he procures at the public storehouses, found in every community, whatever he desires whenever he desires it. This arrangement, you will see, totally obviates the necessity for business transactions of any sort between individuals and consumers."

Bellamy even envisioned that to make a credit card work in the year 2000, the retailer would need to keep a copy of the receipt.

> "The duplicate of the order," said Edith as she turned away from the counter, after the clerk had punched the value of her purchase out of the credit card she gave him, "is given to the purchaser, so that any mistakes in filling it can be

easily traced and rectified."

One thing Bellamy did get wrong, however, was who would pay the bills in 2000. The monthly bills on Bellamy's credit card were not paid by the time-travelling Julian West, but by the US government whose full force and power, the book, were used to pay for its citizens' needs and wants.

While Bellamy did get that fact wrong, it is possible that his novel did actually lead to the creation of the credit card.

Sometime between 1888 and 1890, James Congdell Fargo took a trip from his hometown of Buffalo, New York to Europe. J.C. Fargo (as he was known) was a well-read man. It is possible he had read, perhaps on the long boat trip across the Atlantic, Bellamy's book.

Once in Europe, Fargo found it very difficult to obtain cash. As was typical for travelers in those days, Fargo had carried with him letters of credit. He was a rich and a well-known man. He had founded American Express (then a parcel delivery company) and Wells Fargo (then a regional carrier in California). His letters of credit, however, were of no use to him in most European cities. Outside the biggest cities, merchants and banks simply looked at the letters of credit with confusion and refused to give Fargo the money he needed to enjoy his vacation.

Upon his return from Europe, an irate Fargo ordered American Express executives to solve this problem. To solve it, American Express in 1891 introduced the American Express Traveler's Check. With a traveler's check, all Fargo would have to do is to show up at the local post office, all of which had dealings with American

Express and trusted its credit, to obtain the cash he needed.

Since the Traveler's Check was the world's first real charge card, it is broadly accepted that without it payment cards as we know them would not exist. The impact of Traveler's Checks, however, is not just in getting the ball rolling on the entire payment card industry. In 1957, nearly a century after the Traveler's Checks were introduced, the team in charge of Traveler's Check created the first broadly accepted charge card in the world.

Though Diner Club had launched in 1950 (more on this below), it was America Express's entry into this market in 1957 that spurred the creation of two major products that would go on to become MasterCard and Visa. It was also this American Express team that formed First Data – now the world's largest payment processor.

Early Retail Cards

It is difficult to place a precise date on the invention of retail credit in the United States. It is possible, however, that retail credit predates the US Civil War for a few reasons.

A book written in 1915 by Ben Blanton entitled *Credit, Its Principles and Practice, A Practical Work for Credit Men* suggested that by 1915, the practice of retail credit was at least a few decades old. In fact, the first chapter of the book is dedicated to convincing the reader that the "old methods" were no longer working in 1915 and that it was time to adopt the modern "scientific basis".

A pamphlet distributed in 1917 by the National

Association of Credit Men shows the group's seal indicating that the group was founded in 1896 with simply one word as its motto: vigilance.

It is almost certainly the case that the National Association of Credit Men was founded at least some years after its New York counterpart the Associated Retail Credit Men of New York City; however, the date for the formation of the New York group is difficult to determine.

Regardless, it is safe that assume by the late 1800s there were so many men, as they were mostly men, employed by retailers to work in their credit departments that there was a need for a national lobbying group to represent these men.

Going back even further, we know that starting in 1807 Cowperwaite and Sons, a furniture retailer in New York City, was selling its furniture to local buyers on installment.

By the mid-1800s, Singer Sewing Machine Company was selling tens of thousands of sewing machines to American families on credit. By 1876, Singer had sold 2 million sewing machines in America, nearly all on credit.

While it is difficult to pinpoint the exact date on which the first retail credit purchase was made, it is easy to tell that by the early 1900s Americans loved retail credit. During the first half of 1930, for example, approximately only 45% of all department store purchases in the United States were made by cash or check. The remaining 55% of the purchases were made on credit.

Of course, in the 1800s the customer credit accounts were not accompanied by payment cards. They were simply charges kept on a book with the customer's name next to them.

Cards came into vogue in 1914 when large retailers gave credit cards to their customers. These were simple paper cards that would help cashiers recognize the customers so that the customer would not need to make the trip to the credit counter where the credit book was kept.

While retailers could afford to have such cards outstanding with no expiry dates, oil companies could not. A retailer would know his or her regular clients much better and could simply tell whether the person presenting Joe Smith's card was actually Joe Smith. A gas station attendant, however, saw many times more clients each day. Therefore, the paper cards that were issued by oil companies did have a expiry date. Every three or six months, a customer would have to speak with the gas station manager to get a new card.

These oil cards were incredibly popular. By the mid-1930s, for example, the State of Indiana had nearly 3.5 million residents living in approximately one million households. During that time, nearly 40% of American households owned an automobile. That means that in mid-1930s nearly 400,000 households in Indiana owned an automobile. During this same period, Standard Oil of Indiana distributed nearly 250,000 payment cards in the state – meaning 6 out of 10 people in Indiana that could possibly have an oil payment card had one from Standard Oil.

Obviously, Standard Oil's competitors also issued cards. It is, therefore, safe to assume that during this period nearly every single American with an automobile had a credit card that would allow them to buy oil and services from the gas station during the course of a month, receive one bill, and to pay that bill without any interest at the end of the month.

Unlike retailers, oil companies did not need to worry about customer's having bad credit as frequently. In early 1900s, merely having an automobile was a sign of wealth and good credit. Since everyone who drove to a gas station to buy gasoline owned an automobile, the oil companies simply issued a card to every single customer without having to worry about payments.

By 1930, however, even oil card programs had become subject to fraud. A article titled "Oil Men Jumpy over Credit Cards" in a November 1929 issue of BusinessWeek told a story of a man who began earning a living by carrying passengers between New York and California for less than bus fare. He spent more than $500 (nearly $10,000 in 2017 dollars) on his oil card before the oil company caught on to his fraud. By then, however, he had been jailed for a separate crime and the oil company was not able to recover its loss.

The next major change in payment cards happened in Boston, of course.

In 1928, Farrington Manufacturing Company of Boston began distributing charge-plates. These charge-plates, unlike the earlier paper cards, were very difficult to fraudulently duplicate. They looked like military ID badges embossed on a metal plate.

More importantly, these charge plates removed the need for a credit office in stores. At the point of sale, a cashier could simply take the customer's charge-plate, insert into a machine called an imprinter, and stamp the charge-plate's information (such as the account number and the customer's name) onto the sales slip. This sales slip could then at the end of the day be batched with all the other sales slips and sent to a central credit office as opposed to having to be run to the store's own credit office during every purchase to seek approval of the sale.

By the mid-1930s, many retailers having such charge-plate programs had banded together so that each retailer would accept any charge-plate from any other retailer in the same group. The largest of such groups was the Retail Service Bureau of Seattle which by 1936 had signed up more than a thousand retailers to its joint charge-plate program.

By 1947, virtually all the major department stores in New York had joined together in a similar program. A customer with a charge-plate from Saks could spend money at Arnold Constable, Bloomingdale's, Gimbel's, and Franklin Simon.

While these cooperative charge-plate programs were useful, they were not universal. One could not simply walk into a corner store and buy something using a Saks charge-plate.

Charg-It

The world's first universal card program was launched without much fanfare in Flatbush in 1947. Flatbush was a prominently working class neighborhood in the borough of Brooklyn in New York City. Its residents were mostly Irish-Americans, Italian-Americans and Jewish-Americans. They were not the rich businessmen of Manhattan. They didn't cheer for Joe DiMaggio and the Yankees. They cheered for Duke Snider, the "Duke of Flatbush", who was the Brooklyn Dodger's centerfielder. They didn't have summer homes like the rich families of Manhattan and they didn't frequently find themselves outside Brooklyn.

It was in this neighborhood that John Biggins launched Charg-It. Charg-It was a credit card with every major feature of today's credit cards. It was not a retail card. It was a card backed by the full faith and credit of Flatbush National Bank of Brooklyn. It was accepted nearly everywhere in Flatbush and it was used by nearly everyone who banked at Flatbush National Bank, which in 1947 was the primary bank for everyone in Flatbush.

But Charg-It was an invention of Brooklyn, not Manhattan. People using it were not the most affluent people in the city. Bloomingdale's and Saks had no reason to accept Charg-It as a method of payment. Even Gimbel's, which catered to less wealthy clients, didn't have a business-need to accept Charg-It. After all, Gimbel's of 1930s was located in Herald Square in Manhattan, not in Brooklyn. Furthermore, Gimbel's may not have been keen to have its middle class customers exposed to the immigrants coming in from Flatbush with their Charg-It cards. After all, in the 1940s Gimbel's was fighting long and hard to avoid hiring African-Americans in its New York stores. It is hard to imagine it wanting a group of immigrants trekking to its stores.

While Charg-It was eventually able to expand beyond Brooklyn, attract wealthier clients, it was not able to do so before a wealthy Manhattaneite took over the world with his claim to have invented the world's first universal card program.

In payments, to the victors go the spoils. Thus, very few people remember Charg-It and John Biggins.

Diners Club

Quite a few people, however, do know the payment world's "First Supper".

As the story goes, one evening in 1949, business executive Frank McNamara was having dinner with some of his friends. When the bill for the dinner arrived, McNamara realized that he did not have enough money to pay the bill. The banks were closed and there was no way to get more money until the next morning. An embarrassed McNamara, the legend goes, called his wife who brought the money to pay for the bill. This embarrassing event set Frank McNamara on a course to create the world's first credit card, Diners Club.

Unfortunately, like many things that everyone knows as true, this story is almost certainly false.

First, Frank McNamara was the CEO of the Hamilton Credit Corporation – a very large retail finance company. He did not need an unpaid bill to give him the inspiration to create a credit card program. Second, nearly all restaurants frequented by business executives in Manhattan in the late 1940s would have had charge accounts for their customers similar to the ones present at department stores. All McNamara would have had to do to pay the bill was simply open up a charge account. Third, Diners Club was founded not by McNamara alone but by four well-suited executives. The other three founders were Matty Simmons, who had been a public relations executives for restaurants and nightclubs, Alfred Bloomingdale, whose family owned one of the biggest retail companies in the world, and Ralph Schneider,

McNamara's personal attorney.

Regardless of its starting story, Diners Club made some very important decisions in its early operations. First, Diners Club focused exclusively on restaurants in Manhattan. This meant that its cards would only be attractive to the relatively wealthy portion of the population who lived in Manhattan and had enough wealth to be able to afford to eat at restaurants with some frequency. Another group of high frequency users were salespeople in New York whose job involved taking clients out for dinner and drinks. These salespeople would frequently have to pay for dinners with their own money and would welcome an opportunity to simply hand the monthly bill their bosses.

Second, unlike Charg-It and other card programs, Diners Club charged the businesses who accepted its cards a very high fee. This fee was initially set at 7% of each transaction. Restaurants in Manhattan were happy to pay this amount since they were used to paying hotels and travel agents who sent customers to them a 10% referral fee.

Thus, in 1950, a year after the company's founding, the Diners Club credit card was introduced to the public. In its first moth of operations, Diners Club cards were used to spend $2,000 in New York restaurants – equivalent to almost $15,000 in 2017 dollars. From that spending, McNamara and his three co-founders made less than $200.

It was by no means clear that Diners Club would be a success. In fact, in 1951 after a year of growth, Diners Club had lost nearly $300,000 (nearly $2.5 million in 2017 dollars.) It was this loss that caused McNamara, who owned 70% of the company, to sell his shares to

Bloomingdale and Schneider.

Over the course of the next seven years, Diners Club expanded beyond New York restaurants. By 1957, when American Express launched its own charge card, Diners Club cards were accepted in restaurants, hotels, bars, and airlines all over the United States and Europe.

Interestingly, the first Diners Club cards were not really cards. They were books that listed some information about the card holder and a list of places where the cards could be used. It wasn't until the late 1950s that Diners Club issued its first stand-alone card and not until 1960s that it issued its first plastic card. By 1960s, however, Diners Club and all its copycat companies such as Trip Charge, Golden Key, Gourmet Club, Esquire Club, and Carte Blanche had been overtaken by a much larger payment card company – one that dominates our payment world to this day, Visa (then known as BankAmericard).

Fresno Drop

On September 17, 1958 fewer than one million modern, universal credit cards existed in America. By 1970, more than 100 million credit cards were in the wallets of American consumers.

Those 100 million credit cards changed the face of US payments forever; but the fact that the country was about to change went unnoticed on September 18, 1958. It went unnoticed in New York. It went unnoticed in Boston. It even went unnoticed in Fresno, California – the epicenter of the credit card earthquake that was about to shake America. The Fresno Bee, the small city's daily newspaper, barely covered the news of what had happened.

In the two weeks before September 18, 1958, over 60,000 households in Fresno had found in their mailboxes a thick, brown envelope.

Inside the envelope, there was a plastic card with the bold letters "BankAmericard" printed on it in blue and gold. "Bank" in blue, "Americard" in gold.

Below those letters, a nine-digit account numbers had been embossed into the plastic. Beside those digit the letters "Mar 59" were embossed, below these was written "good thru" in a gold color matching the logo. Below this, the name and the address of the receiver was embossed. At the bottom of the card, the receive would find, printed in blue italics were the words "Bank of America Charge Account Plan."

Without asking for it, and without knowing what it was, nearly all of the residents of Fresno, California, had received a credit card with a $300 spending limit from Bank of America.

On September 18, all of these cards went live. Card holders didn't have to call Bank of America to activate the cards. They didn't have to do anything. They simply had to show up to any store in Fresno and use their cards. They could spend the money without any worry, and if they didn't have enough money to pay the account off at the end of the month they were charged 18% annual interest.

Bank of America wasn't the first bank to try to create a credit card program. Many others had tried and failed. The banks simply could not convince enough Americans to apply for the cards and enough merchants to accept the card.

Bank of America had seen these bank programs start and fail. That's why it picked Fresno, California as its starting place. Fresno was an isolated city. If the program was a massive failure, very few people outside Fresno would notice. Bank of America's reputation would not be harmed greatly. As importantly, given Fresno's size and isolation, the bank could spend months in the lead up to September 1958 convincing merchants that they would sell more product and have an easier time collecting their money if they accepted Bank of America's new card program.

By September 1958, nearly all merchants in Fresno had signed up to accept BankAmericards. By the time the envelopes arrived in Fresno, over 300 merchants had signed up and agreed to pay $25 per month to rent the imprinters needed to copy the BankAmericards. They all had also agreed to pay 6% of each sale to Bank of America – believing that the Bank would drive customers to their stores in the lead up to the Christmas holidays.

Having solved the first problem, i.e. getting merchants, Bank of America attacked the second problem, i.e. getting customers to apply for the card. It simply decided that it didn't need anyone to apply. It didn't need to do a credit check. It simply sent every household in Fresno, California a card and hoped for the best. It was perhaps helpful that the team of people in charge of BankAmericard at Bank of America had come from the bank's internal think-tank rather than from its loan department. It is hard to imagine any loan manager approving loans for people about whom the bank knew next to nothing.

Thus, with the thump of a thick brown envelope started

America's credit card revolution. Within three months of the Fresno Drop, as it became known, Bank of America was handing out tens of thousands of cards in San Francisco and Sacramento and tens of thousands more were arriving in the mailboxes of people in Los Angeles. By October 1959, almost exactly a year after the September 1958 drop. Bank of America had put 2 million credit cards into people's wallets and had singed up over 20,000 merchants all over California to accept these cards. In less than a year, a bank that had no credit card program ended up more than tripling the total number of credit cards outstanding in the United Sates.

One would think that having seen this success, other banks would follow Bank of America's lead. Yet, no one did. No other bank followed Bank of America's aggressive lead into the universal credit card world.

Most other bank CEOs looked at what Bank of America was doing and said, "no thanks!". At the time, their response must have seemed reasonable. In its first year of operations, nearly 22% of people who had used a BankAmericard did not pay their bills. In 1959, Bank of America lost nearly $20 million in its BankAmericard division ($167 million in 2017 dollars.)

While other banks ran away from this business, Bank of America doubled down in 1960. It wasn't until the mid-1960s that other banks realized that Bank of America was building a massive business for itself by accepting the early losses and by then Bank of America have started selling its BankAmericard program to other banks outside California so they could send out BankAmericards to their clients.

By 1970 all the banks that were issuing BankAmericards joined together to form the National BankAmericard Inc.

From that point this company would manage the technology running BankAmericard program for all of its member banks.

A year earlier, seeing the BankAmericard success, United California Bank, Wells Fargo, Crocker National Bank and Bank of California formed the Interbank Card Association to launched their join card program. Interbank called its card MasterCharge.

1977 BankAmericard was renamed the Visa. In 1979, Interbank changed its name to MasterCard.

Today, in 2017, Visa is one of the world's largest companies with a market capitalization of over $200 billion. MasterCard has a market capitalization of nearly $130 billion. Each of them is larger than all but a handful of US banks. Combined together, they would be the most valuable financial company in the world.

Debit Cards

As BankAmericard was establishing its presence across the United States, another technological advancement changed the history of money in the United States.

In 1968, after moving five times in 12 years, Don Wetzel was tired of selling IBM products and being on the road. He quit his job and joined a few other ex-IBM employees at a newly formed company called Docutel.

Shortly after joining Docutel, Don Wetzel found himself waiting in a line at a bank in Dallas, Texas where Docutel was headquartered. Like every other American in 1968, Don Wetzel must have been accustomed to waiting in lines at the banks.

This time, however, something bothered him about the wait. Immediately after the trip to the bank, Wetzel walked into the Docutel office and told his colleagues that he thought Docutel could build a machine that would, according to him, "perform at least 90 percent, perhaps more than 90 percent, of all the transactions processed by a teller."

Within a few months, Don Wetzel and his team had developed the world's first ATM machine and within a year, on September 2, 1969, the first ATM machine was installed at a Long Island branch of Chemical Bank.

Within a year of that first machine, nearly every bank in the United States wanted a Docutel ATM. By the end of 1970, Docutel had so many orders that its delivery time for new machines had extended to more than 30 months.

Within a decade, nearly every bank in the United States had an ATM machine. By 1985, there were nearly as many ATM machines in the United States as there bank branches. By 2002, there were 352,000 ATMs in the United States, nearly five times the number of bank branches in the United States.

While ATM machine have proven to be highly successful, another innovation made by Docutel in the invention of the ATM machine is even more prevalent today.

In 1968, it was not at all clear how the bank cards could be read by ATM machines. All bank cards and credit cards of the era, including the BankAmericards, were read at point of sales by imprinters - by then called zip-caps for the noise they made or knuckle-busters given the frequency with which the user would harm his or her knuckles using the contraption. These machines were not all that different from the imprinters that had been introduced in retail shops alongside charge-plates in the late 1920s.

But the imprinters could not work with a digital machine. To allow the machine to read the card, Docutel needed to store data such as account number, checking account number, savings account number, credit card account number, the bank's routing number and the customer's name. It also had to store this information in a way that could not be read by any machine that a fraudster might create.

To solve this problem, the team at Docutel took an already existing technology, the magnetic tape, and married it to the payment card. The magnetic stripe, now omnipresent on all payment cards, did not exist before 1969.

The early cards used in the Docutel ATMs were not, of course, debit cards. There was no way for any ATM to know whether a bank account had any money left in it or not. The cards used in the ATMs were credit cards that had a strict daily spending limit. It was not until 1972 that debit cards were introduced to the United States. By then, the Docutel ATMs installed in the bank branch were able to communicate with the bank's computer system so that the amount of money given to each customer could be immediately subtracted from his or her bank account.

Even then, these early cards could not be used inside stores as debit cards. It wasn't until 1976 that the first electronic point of sale systems were installed in stores. Debit cards only became usable inside stores when Angelo's and Starmarket, grocery chains located in

Massachusetts, installed new systems that would allow their systems to communicate through a third party with the banks.

It is hard to exaggerate the importance of debit cards and ATMs in the United States today, but in 1970, over a third of American households did not have a bank account. These people were not underbanked by necessity. They simply chose not to have a bank account.

Before the wide prevalence of ACH payments (as outlined above) and debit cards, it was just not that difficult for an American household to go about life without a bank account. A worker would simply get paid in cash or with a check. There would be no need to deposit that check into a bank account since the local department store would gladly cash the check for free; and the local department store was open for business far longer than the local bank branch.

Why would a family who didn't need a mortgage open up a bank account if opening up a bank account required standing in lines to deposit checks, to get cash, and to pay bank fees?

Banks saw this attitude towards their services and tried to offer the ATM and the debit card as their answer. With an ATM, there would be no operating hours. There would be no lines.

And the new ATMs, like the human tellers before them, had to have names. First National Bank called their ATM Tillie the Teller and boasted that "she's a bubbly, giggly kind of character." The bank even held birthday parties for Tillie full with her own personalized "For She's a Jolly Good Teller" recorded song. Other banks named also named their ATMs. An August 8, 1977, issue of New York Times boasted that banks had given their ATM machines a wide variety of names; from the creepy Miss X to the loveable Buttons.

As ATMs became more present across the United States, more and more Americans found a need to carry with them a debit card; but it took some time for debit card transactions to take off as many had envisioned.

For the first decade of their existence, debit cards were used only in local pilots; such as those launched in Angelo's grocers in late 1970s. Even by the early 1990s, over half of the debit cards in the United States were still held by California residents and debit card use fell far behind cash (which still accounted for more than half of the transactions in the United States), check (which accounted for nearly a quarter of transactions), and credit cards (which accounted for about a fifth of the transactions).

In 1990, there were fewer than 300 million debit card transactions in the United States. That's fewer than 2 transactions per person per year or less than 2 out of every 100 transactions at retail stores for the year.

Then something magical happened in the 1993. That year, buoyed by a late 1980s ruling that ATMs did not count as branches and were thus not subject to strict federal regulations, the number of ATMs and debit terminals in stores skyrocketed. In 1992, there were fewer than 100,000 debit terminals in the United States. By 1994, there were nearly 400,000 such terminals.

By 1993, the number of debit transactions had increased to nearly 800 million per year. By 2000, Americans used their debit card 8.3 billion times. By 2003 that number had doubled to 15.6 billion transactions. By 2012, the number had tripled to 47 billion transactions. In fact, today more retail transactions are completed using debit cards than any other method of payment.

In 2016, Americans used their debit cards nearly 70 billion times (compared to fewer than 40 billion credit card transactions). That's nearly 250 transactions per US person per year; a more than 100-fold increase since 1990.

5 DIGITAL CURRENCY & BLOCKCHAIN

In 1990, as Americans were starting to become more comfortable with the idea of using a debit card and before many of them had even heard of the Internet, an eccentric American inventor named David Chaum incorporated a company called DigiCash to completely re-imagine how money works.

Nearly a decade earlier, while Chaum was a PhD student at the University of California, Berkley, he had written a paper titled "Blind Signatures for Untraceable Payments". The paper imagined "a new kind of cryptography" allowing for a "realization of untraceable payments systems" whose main feature would be "increased personal privacy."

After leaving the academic world, Chaum funded DigiCash to commercialize his academic work.

The idea was simple: DigiCash would create an electronic payment system that allowed a user to withdraw money from a bank, encrypt it as a note, and send it to an end recipient. DigiCash payments, the company promised, would be completely private since only the sender and the receiver would have the necessary cryptographic keys.

To simplify it, these cryptographic keys would allow the sender of money to encrypt a string of plain text containing information about the transaction into something completely indecipherable. Then, using decryption keys, the receiver of the transaction could take that unintelligible text and make sense of it again. Private keys would allow users to both encrypt payment information and also add a unique identifying qualifier that proved users were who they said they were.

DigiCash worked with a digital currency called "CyberBucks", and users could buy them using notes and a unique private key. After six years of development, DigiCash signed a deal with Mark Twain Bank headquartered in Ladue, Missouri that would allow people all over the world to open up so called "WorldCurrency" accounts in the bank which could then be used to fund a user's CyberBucks transactions.

As Mark Twain Bank stated in its press release in 1996, DigiCash transactions would be "just like withdrawing money from an account at an ATM or teller window and spending the money at stores."

Within the first year of its operations, nearly 1,000 customers and merchants had opened up DigiCash accounts allowing them to transact with each other. Since e-mail was not yet broadly used, in order to open up an account each customer would have to ask for an application to be mailed to them, which they would then fill out and mail back to Mark Twain Bank; and since web banking had not yet been invented to pay for items a user would have to call the bank and ask to have some money moved to their DigiCash account before opening up the DigiCash provided software to start any transaction.

In 1998, less than two years after its launch and with very few successful transactions, DigiCash filed for bankruptcy.

While DigiCash was not a commercial success, its founding and operations gave rise to a great deal of debate in cryptography message boards and forums of the day. Academics, computer scientists and cryptographers would argue for years about various benefits and flaws of DigiCash.

One of the people debating the benefits of DigitCash was Nick Szabo, a digital currency researcher who ran a popular blog theorizing on the potential development of cryptography.

In 1994, Szabo penned a blog proposing the idea of smart contracts, which would leverage digital currency and cryptography to create computer programs that could carry out transactions.

Szabo argued that because digital currency fulfilled all the necessary requirements for a transaction automatically—verifying identity and funds while remaining secure—in theory, smart contracts could let developers create computer programs that would automatically execute transactions that would only trigger based on a set of rules. One example Szabo used was car leasing.

> "If a loan was taken out to buy that car, and the owner failed to make payments, the smart contract could automatically invoke a lien, which returns

control of the car keys to the bank. This smart lien might be much cheaper and more effective than a repo man. Also needed is a protocol to provably [sic] remove the lien when the loan has been paid off, as well as hardship and operational exceptions. For example, it would be rude to revoke operation of the car while it's doing 75 down the freeway."

Soon after the idea of digital currencies and smart contracts was proposed by Szabo and others, a small group of researchers became obsessed with the idea. The concept of a digital currency free from the binds of governments and central banks, which could be used by anyone across the world, was profoundly interesting.

Over the course of the next decade, many researchers published papers arguing whether people would ever actually use such a digital currency. After all, DigiCash had been a commercial failure at least partially because not many people were interested in paying for things with a digital currency.

Bitcoin

This debate continued in various forums, until October 2008 when an anonymous researcher or a group of researchers published a paper titled "Bitcoin: A Peer-to-Peer Electronic Cash System".

Writing under the assumed name of Satoshi Nakamoto, the author of the paper argued that there were three reasons why a digital currency would succeed.

First, Nakamoto argued that "commerce on the Internet has come to rely almost exclusively on financial institutions" and thus commerce was harmed because of "[increased] transaction costs" that would go along with a financial institution handling transactions.

Second, "non-reversible transactions are not really possible" and thus every merchant would have to assume that a certain amount of fraud is unavoidable. This, obviously, increases the costs of goods and services.

Third, commerce is harmed because of the increased cost of transactions and an entire category of commerce, namely "small casual transactions" where the minimum transaction size is low are not possible.

Thus, bitcoin was born. As proposed by Nakamoto, bitcoin was a digital currency that emulated gold—it had a limited supply, which would make it a scarce commodity over time; it was a payment that would not be controlled by a government or a central authority; and it would be a currency that would become more valuable in the long run.

The primary feature of bitcoin, as envisioned by Nakamoto, would be that it could not be controlled by any one financial institution. Unlike DigiCash, which was practically controlled by one bank, bitcoin would be settled on a so-called distributed ledger.

In order to understand the ingenuity of a distribute ledger, it is important to remember how ACH transactions are settled in the United States.

As noted earlier in the book, since its earliest day ACH transactions have been cleared through a centralized system. That means that each transaction is sent by the bank to a clearing house, in the early days the Federal Reserve of San Francisco and today the Federal Reserve or the Clearing House. Each clearing house maintains on its book a ledger that shows where the money came from and where it was sent. This is how the system ensures that no money is lost and that money is not sent or received twice. Credit cards, debit cards, and checks work similarly. Each transaction is entered onto a ledger sometimes at a bank, like in the debit card system, or another central authority, like the clearing houses.

These one ledger, or centralized ledger, systems therefore by necessity rely on financial institutions. Bitcoin, by design, is meant to avoid financial institutions. In the world of bitcoin, the ledger is shared among everyone in the bitcoin network. This is known as a distributed ledger or a blockchain.

All confirmed transactions, in the world of bitcoin, are included in the blockchain. The question, then may be reasonably asked, how are transactions themselves done?

As was the case with of DigiCash, anyone wanting to use bitcoin must have a special bitcoin account. This account is frequently called a wallet. Each wallet has a secret private cryptographic key that is unique to it. This key is used to confirm that a transaction being sent by a wallet holder is genuine and not fraudulent.

Unlike the single ledger world, however, transactions in the bitcoin network, are not kept between the two parties and the bank. Every transaction in the bitcoin world is broadcast between all the users. This is necessary since every member of the bitcoin world can maintain the ledger of all transactions and transactions on the ledger are updated by broadcasting them through a process called mining.

Mining is the system to used to confirm that a broadcasted transaction is on the blockchain. With mining, all the computers involved in the bitcoin network can agree that a given transaction has taken place at a given time. However, unlike in the banking system, there is no set fee for a transaction paid by the receiver or sender of the transaction. In the bitcoin world, mining is done by computers all over the world which place transactions in so-called blocks based on cryptographic rules. In order to make this process profitable for those who own these mining computers, the bitcoin network creates a lottery that gives miners a fraction of a bitcoin for every transaction that has been confirmed or placed on the blockchain.

As is obvious with the above description, bitcoin is not like other forms of currency. It is unique as a payment method, a form of currency, and in how it deals with monetary policy.

Transactions in bitcoin happen very differently due to the currency's digital nature. Transaction costs are initially miniscule. Miners would get to pick which transactions they would confirm, and would usually do it on a first-come-first-serve basis. Yet, after the mining reward was reduced, as stipulated by Nakamoto's white paper, transaction fees have been increasing. This increase, while not designed specifically in the original bitcoin paper, has happened because users who want their transactions confirmed more quickly pay an additional fee to further incentivize miners. As the mining reward grows smaller, many believe that transaction fees will increase.

Also, unlike regular currency, bitcoins don't actually

change hands during the course of payment. There is a set number of bitcoins at any given time. Instead of electronically moving bitcoins from one wallet to another, the ownership change is simply placed within the blockchain database.

Because the bitcoin blockchain stores information permanently and is irrefutable, the ownership record that lives in the bitcoin blockchain is even more important. If there's any dispute on the bitcoin network, the nature of a blockchain database ensures that there's no doubt as to who owns a bitcoin—there's a permanent ownership record that you can check. This not only limits theft, but also avoids any concern that a user may attempt to spend the same digital currency twice.

Bitcoin is also the first digital currency that deals with monetary policy and the first currency of any kind to use computer code to solve monetary policy. Historically, central banks have dealt with problems like inflation, interest rates, and other fiscal issues through human decision making. Yet, when Nakamoto wrote the white paper and created the bitcoin network, he added monetary policy into bitcoin's code. This means that all future changes to monetary policy are already known and cannot be reversed without a democratic vote of all the major stakeholders.

This preordained monetary policy means that bitcoin can avoid the problems that beset early American currency. If voters could have enforced the promise of Massachusetts government to limit the printing of money, they would have. If Congress could have been limited in printing continentals, much misery might have been avoided.

While bitcoin avoids some of the problems of traditional

currency, it does have its own issues.

One of the problems for a decentralized currency is that when decisions need to be made, there's no central authority to push the consensus one way or another. It is important to remember that unlike DigiCash, bitcoin is not a business or an organization. Bitcoin is an open-source software protocol with no board of directors or a governing authority. Changes in the structure of bitcoin can only be adopted through consensus; and this fact has led to frequent disagreement among the bitcoin community about how the currency should grow and which rules should be adopted.

This, as is easy to imagine, can lead to debate and controversy. For example, should bitcoin participants do anything to make bitcoin transactions faster? Under its original proposal, a bitcoin transaction would take an average of 10 minutes to be confirmed. There are times, however, when transactions could take up to an hour. By comparison a cash transaction takes no time at all and a credit card transaction can take anywhere from two to 20 seconds to process. If transactions were to be made faster, should the reward given to miners be increased for their work in confirming transactions?

These are all questions that a legacy payment system could decide with relative authority and ease. Visa could simply change the rules with a stroke of its pen or the Federal Reserve could simply implement a new piece of software. With bitcoin, however, these questions take months and months of debate and are often left unresolved.

Price & Usage

According to CoinDesk, a leading bitcoin publication, bitcoin started trading in July 2010 at around $0.06 per bitcoin. Those were the early days of bitcoin and the only people interested in the currency were cryptography enthusiast and computer scientists.

Over the next three years, as interest in bitcoin grew the price of bitcoin increased. In March 2013, one bitcoin was worth $100.

It was around this time that two large events brought even more attention to bitcoin.

Long before Satoshi Nakamoto published the first bitcoin paper, a programmer named Jed McCaleb had built a website focused on allowing users of an online game named Magic: The Online Gathering to buy and sell digital cards. His website, mtgox.com, short for Magic: The Gathering Online eXchange, launched sometime in January 2007. The website didn't receive much traffic and by the end of 2007, McCaleb had all but abandoned the idea for an online card exchange. The site lay dormant promoting McCaleb's various gaming interests until July 2010.

Having read Nakamoto's bitcoin paper, McCaleb had become interested in bitcoin in early 2010 and decided that his old card exchange site could be used to buy and sell bitcoin instead of digital cards. On July 18, 2010, Mt. Gox was launched as one of the world's first bitcoin exchanges.

Given bitcoin's increasing popularity, Mt. Gox quickly became a popular bitcoin exchange; but by January 2011 its founder had already grown tried of dealing with the website that was receiving tens of thousands of dollars, much of it from unknown sources, every week. So on

February 3, 2011 McCalebt sold the business to Mark Karpeles, a French programmer living in Japan.

Perhaps having perfect foresight or perhaps given the uncertainty around bitcoin and legality of the whole ecosystem, McCaleb insisted that the sale document include a clause specifically saying that "the Seller is uncertain if mtgox.com is compliant or not with any applicable U.S. code or statute, or law of any country" and that "the buyer agrees to indemnify Seller against any legal action that is taken against Buyer or Seller with regards to mtgox.com or anything acquired under this agreement."

Having taken over the website, Karpeles began to grow it quickly and within weeks, Mt. Gox was the world's largest bitcoin exchange. Almost immediately, Karpeles became a large name in the bitcoin community and began encouraging the employees he had hired to call him "the king of Bitcoin". (As an aside, I'm the CEO of a company called Kash but have never been able to have my employees call me the King of Kash.)

Yet, even from the first days there were signs that perhaps this bitcoin emperor was lacking some clothing.

Just over two months after he took over Mt. Gox, Karpeles realized that the site was missing nearly 80,000 bitcoins and that it had somehow bean hacked.

Emails, released through court documents, show that in late April 2011 McCaleb urged Karpeles to among other things consider buying the 80,000 bitcoin on the open market at a cost of nearly $63,000. Yet, it seems, Karpeles did nothing in response to finding the 80,000 bitcoins missing. By June 2011, the price of bitcoin had increased so much that to replace the missing 80,000 bitcoins Mt.

Gox would have had to spend over $800,000.

Later that month, in June 2011, Mt. Gox was hacked again. This time, Karpeles responded by the moving majority of the exchange's bitcoin holding into a "cold storage" and placing them into safety deposit boxes in various Japanese banks.

This move made it nearly impossible to reconcile how much bitcoin Mt. Gox owned against how much it was actually supposed to own.

To understand this, it is important to know the difference between "cold storage" and "hot storage". Recall from above that a person's bitcoins are held in what is called a bitcoin wallet.

A wallet with hot storage, or a "hot wallet", is a bitcoin address that is connected to the internet that can spend bitcoin at anytime. A wallet with cold storage, or a "cold wallet", is not connected to the internet. In fact, a cold wallet can be something as simple as a piece of paper that contains all the information needed to generate the private keys necessary to spend bitcoin.

Unlike a hot wallet, a cold wallet cannot be easily hacked; but unlike a hot wallet, it is incredibly difficult to maintain a proper record of all bitcoin held by someone if it is all printed out on various pieces of paper. The move to maintain nearly all of its bitcoin in cold storage meant that Mt. Gox was no longer capable of adequately assessing whether it had all the reserves it needed in order to account for all its purchases and sales of bitcoin.

As bitcoin prices kept rising, Karpeles became more and

more wealthy. By late 2013, Mt. Gox was handling over 70% of the world's bitcoin trade – and this is when big trouble greeted Mt. Gox.

In mid-May 2013, Mt. Gox was sued by its biggest business partner Coinlab for $75 million. As if this wasn't bad enough, days after the Coinlab suit was filed, the US Department of Homeland Security issued a warrant to seize nearly $5 million from Mr. Gox's US payment processor Dwolla. The US government was alleging, among other things, that it was in violation of US Financial Crimes Enforcement Network laws and operating illegally in the United States.

Around this time, Mt. Gox customers began complaining that they were experiencing delays withdrawing their funds from their Mt. Gox accounts.

For the next few weeks, Mt. Gox avoided most press questions and attempted to allow customers to withdraw money in small batches. By late 2013, however, it became clear that Mt. Gox was in serious trouble and protestors began to protest the company's offices in Tokyo.

The trickle of complaints turned into a flood in February 2014 when on February 7, Mt. Gox halted all withdrawals complaining about a "bug in the bitcoin software". Two weeks later, on February 28, Mt. Gox filed for bankruptcy in Japan claiming that hackers had stolen nearly 850,000 bitcoins, worth about $460 million at the time, form the company.

The crash of Mt. Gox over the course of late 2013 to March 2014 caused the price of bitcoin to fall by nearly 50%. In late November 2013, while Mt. Gox was being sued but before its financial troubles, bitcoin was trading at $980. By late March 2014, bitcoin was trading at $450.

While the Mt. Gox bankruptcy was a big shock to the bitcoin community, the network had suffered another devastating blow a few months earlier.

On January 27, 2011, a few days after Jed McCalebt sold Mt. Gox to Mark Karpelès, an anonymous poster named "altoid" wrote a brief post on Shroomery.org, a website dedicated to, in its own words, spreading "accurate information about magic mushrooms so people can make informed decisions about what they put in their bodies."

Altoid, wrote that he had "come across this website called Silk Road" that would "allow you to buy and sell anything online anonymously." Two days later, a user using the same name, posted a similar message on Bitcointalk.org, a website for bitcoin enthusiasts. Within weeks Silk Road, a website accessible only using special browsers so as to hide its tracks and anonymize its visitors, had become popular on both sites. A user on Shroomery.org posted, excitedly, "Yes, you can really buy drugs safely online."

By May 2011, Silk Road was so popular that hundreds of users were buying and selling drugs online – almost completely hidden from the US federal and state governments.

If Silk Road had used credit cards or online payment providers like PayPal to process transactions, all its transactions would have been trackable by banks and the US government.

Bitcoin, however, was readily available in early 2011 and it was different from every other method of payment.

While bitcoin transactions can be tracked, they can also be made pseudo-anonymous. As described earlier, a bitcoin transaction is really a series of transactions and when a bitcoin is spent, the public ledger is adjusted to reference who spent and who received the currency. This information is publicly available, and thus bitcoin transactions are traceable. Unlike a bank account, however, a bitcoin address is not tied to identity of any user. So while it is perfectly obvious which user sent how much bitcoin to which other user, the names of the bitcoin users themselves can be easily hidden. For example, my bitcoin wallet address is 1BN1XUE3P2aSFb77sx8rhAEJ CREbgXcn7F. Without me telling you that right now, there is no way you could know who owns that wallet.

Also, unlike credit card transactions, it is very difficult to trace which computer started a given bitcoin transaction. In today's world, transactions are frequently traced using IP addresses. An IP address is a unique string of numbers that identifies each computer in a network. An IP address is to a computer what a home address is to a house. It is unique. So it can be used to track spending that started on a computer. Bitcoin, however, is designed such that transaction data be transmitted or forwarded to random computers on the network. So while it can be said which computers were involved in a bitcoin transaction, it is practically impossible to tell whether a computer stared, amended or simply forwarded the transaction information.

This pseudo-anonymity means that users on Silk Road could buy and sell things with much more anonymity than they could have if they were using checks, credit cards or even ACH transactions. This feature led to increasing popularity of Silk Road.

By early 2012, Silk Road was on track to do about $15 million in transactions annually. Estimates suggest that an overwhelming portion, perhaps as much as 75%, of this amount was illegal drugs. Although other items for purchase included tutorials on how to hack ATM machines, illegal pornography, and even a hitman to kill your business rival.

As Silk Road grew in popularity, its founder, known as Altoid on Mushroomery.org and believed to be a user named Dread Pirate Roberts on Silk Road, began looking to hire engineers to help improve the website.

In mid-October 2011, Altoid posted on Bitcointalk.org that he was looking for "an IT pro in the Bitcoin community". The job posting asked interested applicants to send an e-mail to "rossulbricht at gmail dot com". This job posting was likely the first time Altoid was related to an account with an actual name behind it – Ross Ulbricht.

As was later proven in a criminal trial, Ross Ulbricht, the founder of Silk Road was a brilliant, libertarian ideologue. He had been a volunteer on and a donor to Ron Paul's campaigns for President. He had written many essays promoting his political ideology.

In one essay, he wrote that "Silk Road is about something much bigger than thumbing your nose at the man and getting your drugs anyway. It's about taking back our liberty and our dignity and demanding justice." And that "the drug war is an acute symptom of a deeper problem, and that problem is the state. If they legalize, regulate and tax it, it's just one more part of society under their thumb, another productive sector that they can leech off of."

In another essay, making an impassioned defense of non-state currencies like bitcoin, Ulbricht wrote that "the Federal Reserve system relies on the force of government to maintain its monopoly power on the issuance of money. This is how all central banks maintain their control. Without the state's involvement, people would be free to use whatever currency they like."

By mid-2011, with his libertarian message and a seemingly unlimited supply of illegal drugs for sale, Ulbricht (through his pseudonym Dead Pirate Roberts) had become a hero in some circles. It was also around this time that the US government began to take the threat of Silk Road seriously.

On June 5, 2011, U.S. Senator Charles Schumer called a press conference to declare that Silk Road had become a public menace.

> "[Silk Road] allows buyers and users to sell illegal drugs online, including heroin, cocaine, and meth, and users do sell by hiding their identities through a program that makes them virtually untraceable," said Senator Schumer "It's a certifiable one-stop shop for illegal drugs that represents the most brazen attempt to peddle drugs online that we have ever seen. It's more brazen than anything else by lightyears."

This began a two-year investigation by the US Drug Enforcement Administration and the FBI which ended on October 2, 2013 in a San Francisco public library when Ulbricht was arrested and charged with drugs trafficking, money laundering and attempted murder (Ublricht had once allegedly attempted to hire a hitman to kill a business associate whom he believed was cooperating with the police).

Two weeks after the arrest, FBI announced that it had seized nearly 144,000 bitcoins, valued at $28.5 million, from Ulbricht.

The Silk Road saga was the most broadly reported coverage bitcoin had received and the currency's affiliation with a criminal enterprise did great harm to bitcoin's value.

The day before Ulbricht's arrest, bitcoin was trading at $145 on Mt. Gox. Immediately after the arrest was announced, its value plummeted to $109 – a fall of nearly 25% - thought the price slowly recovered.

The combination of Mt. Gox and Silk Road along with a lack of general increase in bitcoin transactions caused enthusiasm for bitcoin to be muted for some months.

The price of bitcoin had risen steadily throughout 2013, reaching a high of nearly $1,000 on November 25, 2013; but the price steadily decreased from that point reaching the low of nearly $200 by February 2015.

The price of bitcoin alongside various use cases for the currency and attention from big banks recovered slowly throughout 2016 and crossed the $1,000 mark in early February 2017. As of this writing, in June 2017, the price for a bitcoin is just over $2,800 – an all-time high.

While the price of bitcoin has increased dramatically and quite a few other digital currencies have found their footing, it is unclear whether bitcoin will ever become a mainstream currency.

For those keeping track, it is important to remember that

it took nearly 20 years before debit cards became mainstream in America. By that record, we should not judge bitcoin until nearly 2030.

CONCLUSION

Payments and money are an important part of everyone's day to day life, but they are a part we rarely talk about.

On any given day, the average person pays for what he or she eats, what he or she uses, how he or she gets places, and how he or she lives.

We take our cards out to pay for breakfast, we use checks to pay rent, we use ACH to pay bills, and we use cash to pay the local coffee shop. It is difficult to imagine an average person in the United States going through his or her day without being touched by all forms of payment mentioned above. Even the most digital of us are touched by cash payments – frequently having to wait slightly longer behind someone counting out coins at a cashier. Even the most analog of us are touched by digital payments – frequently having to figure out how to pay for things online.

And everyone is affected by the cost of payments.

Cash, checks, ACH, credit and debit cards, and even digital currencies all have costs associated with them. These costs are eventually paid by the consumer. As an example, the Merchants Payment Coalition estimates that credit and debit card fees alone drive up the prices for everything costing the average family in the United States nearly $400 each year.

That's a $400 payment tax that very few people talk about. By comparison imagine how many newspaper columns would be written if the United States Congress passed a law increasing everyone's property taxes by 20%. (The average American household pays about $2,000 in property taxes.)

Similarly, imagine how many newspaper columns have been written about Amazon's effect on US retail and the ever shrinking US retail margins. How many times have you heard a big retail chain shut its doors because it cannot turn a profit in today's market? We often hear the reasons given as increased competition, higher wages, or increased rent. But for virtually every merchant in the United States payment costs are the second-highest operating expense after labor. How many stores could remain open if costs of payments were lower?

We don't know the answer to these questions because we don't talk about payments that much. There are two reasons we don't talk about payments that much.

First, the technical aspects of payments are incredibly complicated.

The average reader doesn't really know how the internet works. How a computer talks magically with another computer. Same is true for payments. The underlying system is incredibly complicated, so we don't' talk about it that much. Even this book has avoided much of the technical discussion about payment systems. (For an incredibly detailed overview, please read *Payment Systems in the US* by Carol Coye Benson and Scott Loftesness.)

Second, payment and banking in general seem boring at first glace. It is all about numbers, after all.

Once we can get past the initial hesitance, however, the world of payments is fascinating. Payments has a history full of big characters and interesting events that mirror the building of any civilization. How many other issues have given rise to entire political movements? How many other aspects of our lives were hotly debated by America's Founding Fathers and by King George? How many other issues would have gotten attention from titans such as JP Morgan and philosophers like Karl Marx and Adam Smith?

The history of payments is incredibly fascinating. The goal of this book, as stated in the introduction, was to give a cursory review of it. I hope it has accomplished that.

AN INCOMPLETE BIBLIOGRPAHY

This is not an academic work. Much of it has been written from memory. I've attempted to fact check all the facts and the stories – and they all have held true. To extent there are mistakes, as I am sure there are, I will update the digital copy of this book. However, there are certain works and writings without which the writing of this book would have been impossible. This is an incomplete list of such works, listed alphabetically by author's last name.

I will continue to update a bibliography and a reading list on my personal website www.nejatian.com.

Aboucher, R. *Bank Charge Cards in the 1970s*, Banking 1969

Adams, K. *The Bank Card: Yesterday, Today, and Tomorrow*, American Bankers Association 1974

Baker, D. *The Law of Electronic Fund Transfer Systems*, Gorham & Lamont 1988

Batiz-Lazo, B. *A Brief History of the ATM*, The Atlantic 2015

Caskey, J. *Is the Debit Card Revolution Finally Here?*, Federal Reserve 1994

Davies, G. *A History of Money from Ancient Times to the Present Day*, University of Wales 1994

Durkin, T. *Credit Cards: Use and Consumer Attitudes*, 1970–2000, Federal Reserve 2000

Evans, D. *Economics of the Payment Card Industry*, National Economic Research Association 1993

Evans, D. *Paying with Plastic: The Digital Revolution in Buying and Borrowing*, MIT Press 1999

Federal Reserve, *Federal Reserve Payments Study 2016*, 2016

Ferguson, N. *Ascent of Money*, Penguin Books 2008

Friedman, J. *House of Cards: Inside the Troubled Empire of American Express*, Kensington 1992

Friedman, M. *A Monetary History of the United States*, Princeton 1963

Griffith, K. *A Quick History of Cryptocurrencies BBTC — Before Bitcoin*, Bitcoin Magazine 2014

Higgins, S. *3 Pre-Bitcoin Virtual Currencies That Bit the Dust*, Coindesk 2014

Holmes, T. *Debit card statistics*, CreditCards.com 2015

Lord, L. *He Led the 'Charge It' Charge*, U.S. News & World Report 1990

Mandel, L. *The Credit Card Industry: A History*, G.K Hall & Co 1990

Milletti, M. *Banks Promoting A Mechanical Pal*, New York Times 1977

Nakamoto, S. *Bitcoin: A Peer-to-Peer Electronic Cash System*. Bitcoin.org

Rodriguez McRobbie, L. *The ATM is Dead. Long Live the ATM!*, Smithsonian 2015

Rothbard, M. *A History of Money and Banking in the United States*, Ludwig von Mises Institute 2002

Sienkiewicz, S. *Credit Cards and Payment Efficiency*, Federal Reserve 2001

Szabo, N. *Smart Contracts*, 1994

United States Government Accountability Office, *Rising Interchange Fees*, US Congress 2009

Vanatta, S. *Charge Account Banking: A Study of Financial Innovation in the 1950s*, Princeton 2016

ABOUT THE AUTHOR

Kaz Nejatian is the CEO of Kash (kashpayments.com), a payment company with offices in San Francisco, California and Toronto, Canada.

Before co-founding Kash, Kaz was a lawyer in New York city advising financial institutions and retailers on various issues including payment and payment security.

Kaz has been obsessed with payments and banking since he was a teenager working at his family's corner store. He wrote his first payment business plan at the age of 18.

He lives in San Francisco with his wife Candice and spends most of his time taking credit for the amazing work done by his colleagues at Kash.

52806849R00055

Made in the USA
San Bernardino, CA
29 August 2017